dear new york.

dear new york.

a collection of poetry,

letters,

and shorts

by em jenkins.

dear new york.

This book is dedicated to several people and places dear to my heart. To everyone mentioned in this book, whether by name or indirectly, this one is for you.

dear new york.

Letters, I. "Dear New York".

Dear New York,

    It's been awhile since we've spoken. To be honest, I think of you a lot.

    I suppose it's hard for me to put that into words.

    It's funny, right? The way we think about things but cannot fully express our emotions verbally. There's something about feelings that are too fragile to speak or too frail to write upon a page, lest we shatter ourselves and ruin the moment.

    That's my art side talking, though.

    If I'm telling the truth, I've cried a few times since we parted. I remember you like an old friend who took me on adventures and showed me the world, because that's exactly what you did. You taught me things I never knew. You showed me the stars, even when the lights were too bright to physically see them in the night sky.

    Do you miss me like I miss you?

    Probably not.

    You are much to busy to notice I am gone, showing other girls the world like you did for me. It's fair, though. Go on and reveal your thrilling mysteries. Why should I have you all to myself? That would be lackluster and immature, and I only wish to share your beauty with others. I am forever recalling my visits to the streets of my favorite places.

    The sirens were constant.

    They were always ringing in my ears, distracting from the flowers on the streets or the bikers going about their busy days in the rain. How brave they were to venture out in the storms. I could never muster that willpower.

dear new york.

I have been venturing through my own city, recently. Every one way street and pedestrian crowd reminds me of you. Birmingham could never be you, though. She's far too small, and she doesn't have the personality that you do.

You will always have a special place in my heart. Perhaps we could say you were my first love, but that might be too ambitious of a statement, for I am a single girl in a city thousands of miles away.

I want to come back. I long to return to the sights and sounds that I adore, the middle-of-the-night furious road rages and the always-changing traffic light colors.

How is uptown?

How are the parks, the museums, and the Italian restaurants? Are the skies still dreary like they were in July? Does the stifling heat make eighteen thousand people collectively post complaints on social media? Probably not, because it is November, but I remember it like it was yesterday. (Clearly, those people have never experienced a Southern summer.)

I suppose we will find out if we were meant be on December 15th. The date approaches steadily, less than a month and a half away. I can imagine an admissions office full of people reading through the portfolios and essays, the hundreds and hundreds of applicants like me. Dear New York, if you had your way, would you accept all of us? Or are you just as selective as the people in charge? I've only heard tales of those who have failed to succeed, and those who have risen above the challenge. Was it you, or was it someone playing your part?

You are, by far, the most impressive city I have ever visited. Two and a half weeks was not enough time to take in your sights, but at least now I understand why people pay so much to live there. There is something to do, all the time. There is never a dull moment, never a split

dear new york.

second of boredom, unless perhaps it is two in the morning and the only sounds are motorcycles without mufflers and drunk millennials on a Friday night.

On Fifth Avenue is where I truly fell in love. On the streets that ran alongside the beautiful Central Park, I truly began to see myself in the future. The essays asked me where I saw myself in five years, and it was with you. To be with you would be a dream come true, some elaborately-fashioned reality I can only dream of achieving until it becomes true. Do dreams work? I shall find out.

Dear New York, please welcome me. December 15th, you will have your decision. In less than a month and a half, you will either open your arms or lock your doors.

These are the thoughts of a seventeen-year-old romantic, tucked away in her room in Alabama, writing letters to the greatest city in the world.

dear new york.

Poetry, I. "Dear Jessica".

dear jessica, how are you doing in new york?

are the skies cloudy like i remember?

dear friend of mine, how's life on the east shore?

are the breezes still warm in september?

dear jessica, i hear your voice like it was yesterday

when we were walking down amsterdam avenue…

dear friend of mine, i know you're living your best life

i didn't think we'd be like this when i met you.

a thousand miles apart

i still miss you

too many miles apart

do you know how much i miss you?

dear new york.

Letters, II. "To My Old Best Friend".

Do you remember the day it snowed?

It was cold outside, colder than we were used to. I forgot my gloves, so I borrowed your brother's. We took photos, because I was in photography class and my teacher wanted me to bring work in next week. You were gorgeous.

Do you remember being bored out of our minds playing Scrabble the next day? We had a Guardians of the Galaxy film playing in the background, but we ended up turning our full attention to it because the game was idle. We were both good writers, but we had trouble coming up with words.

Is that where we fell short?

You and I were so close. Best friends, inseparable. Always cursing the miles between us - we lived on opposite sides of town, but we kept in contact every minute of every day.

Do you remember the history of our three-hour-long phone calls?

What has happened to us?

Your family is struggling, and so is mine. Somehow, the thing that makes us the same is the thing driving us apart. We are no different, but we have become foes. The mood swings are too much for me to bear - friends one day, at each other's throats the next.

Since when did you speak the language of passive-aggressive?

You were a peacemaker in your younger years.

The world has aged you.

I knew you would change as you grew up, but not like this - you have grown distant, and I feel as if I have only matured. Our paths are separating, forming some sort of gap that we cannot seem to bridge. I hesitate to invite you to my gatherings, because I don't want to crack the eggshells I walk on when I am around you.

Do not mistake my good intentions for insincerity - I think of you in everything I do. Every film club date I set, I make sure it's possible for you to attend. Every party I plan, I do it on a day I know you are free. We have known each other for less than three years, but there is something to do with you in almost everything I do. You are my best friend, even if we have since moved apart.

We are planets moving out of orbit.

Something has shifted in the gravity around us and, naturally, we follow the paths set before us. Our journeys may never be the same again, but I will always be here for you.

I will always support your dreams and your aspirations, and provide advice should you require it.

I will always remember you as the beloved best friend of a lonely extroverted high school freshman.

I will always invite you to my parties.

I will always write of you in positive ways.

I will always think of you.

I will always love you.

Are you crying yet?

dear new york.

Short, I. "Violet"

There was something about Violet Trent that scared the rest of the world.

It was not because of the way she looked. No, Violet Trent was probably one of the most innocent-looking people in all of the country, with her dark hair that fell over her shoulders in waves of mahogany, streaked with blonde from the sunlight she danced in. She was a perfect picture of elegance and class, someone that was looked up to by the younger generation, even though she was hardly eighteen years of age.

It was not because of the way she talked. Her voice had a light air to it, and she sounded the way the ocean does on a calm day, rising and falling with emotion but always remaining stable. There was a reason she was asked to teach the children's classes on Friday mornings. She was trusted by everyone who knew her.

It was definitely not because of the way she stared at the sunset in awe of its beauty, as if her breath had been taken away by the rays of orange and red. And then as night fell, betrayed by the day that had abandoned it, she used to go inside and sit in the windowsill, watching as the stars came out from the safety of her bedroom. She was quiet, not outspoken like her brother. She was not to be feared by anyone or anything, as she was completely harmless.

Except in one way, that was.

The problem was that Violet Trent knew exactly who she was. Now, that was extremely dangerous…for, on Earth, no one was supposed to define themselves. They were to be defined by society and to conform to the rules set before them by other people, not by themselves. Violet Trent was an outsider in this way.

dear new york.

She walked the streets with some sort of pride, something no one else was allowed to have. It was almost sickening to see how happy she was as herself, how excited she was to try new things without the permission of society. They frowned upon her, lashing out with insults meant to snap her into line. They called out her clothing, her hair, her shoes...anything to make her feel like she was less than she believed herself to be. It was difficult for everyone to persuade her to start to back off on her independence, to rely on the world more to make decisions for her. Finally, though, she gave in.

Her hair was the first to go. Its length had been long and wavy, but she cut it to her shoulders. She began to wonder if she had made the right decision, but Violet could never go back, for she had made up her mind. The only way to go back was to go forward and wait for time to do as time usually does.

The second thing changed about her was the fact that she never wore makeup. The truth was that she did not need it, for her features accentuated her beauty perfectly without the need of a colored powder or a lip stain. However, everyone else was wearing it, participating in the trend that wasn't bad but was not meant for her, and she had to give in to their words after they constantly pestered her to join them. She didn't know why she hadn't tried it before as soon as she began.

Within a month, the old Violet Trent had been completely abandoned, and someone new appeared to take her place. There were no complaints, for society was glad she had surrendered and become a part of them. She began to grow her status, meeting new people just for the sake of adding them to her ever-growing friend circle. She made truces with the darkness in order to steadily rise to the top of her group, looking down at everyone else from so high up. She was never going back, she loved this new life. She wondered why she hadn't given in before, why she had resisted for so long when this wondrous world was what she had been resisting. She was never hesitant anymore, always quick to make a decision, confident and bold and brave. People looked up to her to know what was right and wrong, and she gave her best answer every time. She wanted to please everyone and disappoint no one, because that was what she was taught by the people above her. She was rising to their level.

Her family wondered what had happened to the old Violet, though. They might have been the only people who missed her, but they did so with all of their hearts. They begged for her to return to them, for her to turn back to them like she used to. They asked her to teach the children's classes on Friday mornings again, but she dismissed them without saying anything in regards to their wishes. She had turned her back on them while she was turning towards society. She had evolved from the person she used to be into someone she never wished to become. If she could've seen what she would eventually be, she would have said no back in the beginning, but it was too late to do that now. Violet Trent was different now, and that had to be accepted by the people who used to know her.

There was something about Colton Jones that the rest of the world ignored.

It was not because of his smile, dazzling and blindingly white. He would show it off in all the photos on his social media account, waiting for all the likes and comments to roll in as they usually did, coming in the hundreds and thousands. Millions of strangers, viewing him and his smile, and agreeing to see more of him by following. It was so harmonic, but yet it was mayhem. The problem was that society was accustomed to the chaos they had introduced themselves to.

dear new york.

It was not because of his personality. He spoke with such conviction that anything he said would be regarded by even those who didn't necessary like him. His laugh was contagious, and he was fun to be around. There were many that would've given anything to be in his presence for just a few minutes, even a few seconds. He was one of the prominent figures in the media, because he was not only attractive but he was humorous. He was the kind of person anyone would give everything to be.

It was definitely not because of the way he sat on the roof of the apartment building he stayed in some nights, recalling the constellations his mother taught him before her passing. He would stay up there for hours sometimes, never taking his gaze off of the millions of stars that were above his head. He was fascinated by the unknown, drawn in by the possibility of something else. He was the perfect child of the media, and he would stay that way. He was everything society wanted him to become.

Except in one way, that was.

The thing was, the world ignored the fact that he was actually interested in the stars and the ocean and everything nature had to offer, for it spoiled the internet's view of him, and that could never happen in their eyes. They would be making all the decisions, and he would never have a say in his own life. Raised on witty captions and boomerang videos, Colton Jones was captive to the society that created him.

Maybe he wanted to be free from their grasp, though. Maybe he wondered what it would be like to delete it all, to pretend he was someone normal for once. To let the hype surrounding him and his smile die down, to turn down the modeling contract he'd been offered. He'd always wanted to raise a family - a small house in the Californian countryside was just what he needed. He could almost smell the scent of freshly cut grass now, and hear the

dear new york.

laughter of future children. There was no one genuine for him to love, though. Anyone that threw themselves at him were only after him because of his humor and his good looks, and not for everything else that he believed and stood for. He had hundreds of thousands of followers, but he felt completely alone.

He noticed Violet Trent, though. He used to go to school with her, back when she was free from all the oppressing molds the world tried to force on her. She used to have her longer hair and her breezy summer dresses, and those mismatched socks she wore in different colors all through high school. She was the one he would choose to spend the rest of his time with, if he had the choice. Unfortunately for him, Violet was just like everyone else now, one more face in a crowd of thousands.

He reached out to her anyway, though. He messaged her through the social media application, hoping she would see it. He assumed she received hundreds in a day, as he did. He never had time to go through all of his, and he only hoped she would be more diligent in going through hers, for his sake.

It wasn't until four weeks later that a response actually came up in his notifications.

And what he read surprised him.

Violet Trent was tired of trying to be the world's precious starlet. She was giving up giving in, and she wasn't going back. She abandoned her persona and archived all of the photos except the scenic ones that represented who she truly was.

She asked Colton Jones to join her.

He didn't have to think twice. He went through his account and archived everything that didn't really represent who he was. He changed his bio and his profile photo. He stopped trying to please everyone else and worked to do what was best for him.

dear new york.

Colton and Violet were free, and they were the only ones swimming against the current, but they were happy like that.

The future was safe in the hands of the trustworthy and true.

dear new york.

Poetry, II. "Dramatic".

ever since i got back,

i've been missing you.

is there ever going to be a time when i don't?

ever since i got back,

the songs have been playing.

new york on repeat: i could turn it off, but i won't.

you did well convincing me you were perfect

and i'll believe that for the rest of my life.

sunset between buildings,

a street corner somewhere in this foreign land.

your voice in my head,

calling down the winding stairways we walked.

do you think of me like i think of you?

do you fall in love with places you go and people you meet?

do you wish to start over so you can experience it again?

perhaps we should reminisce in what we once had.

ever since i got back,

i've been daydreaming.

new york on repeat: i could regret it, but i don't.

dear new york.

Short, II. "Smoke".

(This story is an edit of a short I wrote in 2015. It is divided into three parts.)

part one.

in which the soldier blames himself for a tragedy that he could not prevent.

It hurt to think about what had just happened.

His hands shook and refused to steady, his nerves walking a tightrope that he himself had suspended. The soldier's eyes roamed the fiery ground, the rubble underfoot trampled by the many boots of survivors.

This is my fault.

Was it his fault?

In his eyes, it definitely was. He had gone off to settle some business with an old friend, and she had insisted on following him. He had warned her that things might get dangerous. And he had let her come along anyway.

It was her choice, but it was his consent. He could have stopped her. He could have. She would have listened to him.

She had always listened to him.

Clouds of ash rose into the air, remnants of the fire that had raged the town moments before. Smoke was nearby, hovering above the place like a thick blanket. Small fires were here and there, but it was nothing compared to the walls of flames that had once been.

A body lay on the ground, that of the man who thought it would be okay to burn the village to the ground. His corpse was mangled and burned, scars creeping up his legs and swelling red marks making his face indistinguishable. Even his family would have a hard time recognizing him.

But he did not care.

The man had set fire to the city. With what had happened at the end of it all, the soldier had every reason to despise the stranger, dead or alive.

And there she was, his beloved, the only one who truly understood him. The only person on the Earth that knew him as more than just a name.

This is my fault.

As he knelt on the ground next to a familiar corpse, his breath caught in his throat.

She was lovely, even in death, but it was hard for him to breathe knowing that this was his fault. He brushed a hand over her cheek, trying to choke back any sobs that threatened to erupt. Her auburn hair was full of ash and debris from being thrown to the ground, and her lips had gone pale. She was still, stiff, lifeless.

Pulling the body closer to him, he couldn't feel a heartbeat. He'd known that he wouldn't be able to, but after sensing her pulse so many times before, it felt wrong and irregular.

Sebastian Gulinov sat on the ground inside a town of ruins, rocking the still figure of Natalia Abernathy back and forth, trying not to cry as he blamed himself repeatedly for her death.

part two.

in which the woman finds herself hemmed in between worlds, the decision her own.

"Hello, Natalia."

dear new york.

The dark haired woman spun around, trying to see where the soft voice had come from. It was a girl's voice, a child's. Her eyes found the being and studied her.

"Only one person calls me that, and you're not him."

The young girl that Natalia was studying had blonde hair, so blonde it was almost white. Her eyes were blue as the sky, and her dress was golden, tied with a red sash.

The girl offered Natalia a smile, as if Natalia understood nothing but would learn soon. "Oh, Natalia," she said, suddenly frowning, her eyes distant. "You are not supposed to be here. Unless, of course," she hurried to add, "you wish to be."

Natalia made a slow circle, studying where she was. White surrounded her, but blackness beyond a corridor made her shiver. She faced the girl. "Where am I, then?"

The girl shook her head. "I can't say. But you have a choice to make. You can stay here, or..."

She paused, her words trailing off. Natalia motioned with her hand for the girl to continue.

"Or you could return to him."

Him.

The girl waved her hand, and a projection appeared in midair. Natalia could see her husband hunched over, perhaps even crying. He only ever cried around her, and only a few times. Then she realized that he was around her, or her body, at least.

Staring at herself was stranger than she thought it'd be. She self-consciously picked at her hair after seeing cinders in it in the projection. She came up empty, as her dark locks in this place were clean and straight.

"Am I...dead?"

dear new york.

The girl waved her hand again, and the projection disappeared. "What is the last thing you remember?"

"A man. His name was...well, I can't remember. But he set fire to a town, and I volunteered to help move out victims from houses whilst Sebastian worked on extinguishing the fire. I was in a house with a small child, when it blew. I passed out."

"And?"

"And I woke up, here."

The girl frowned again, and the muscles in her face pulled her expression into one of confusion. "That's odd. That should not have happened. You were supposed to survive the explosion."

"Survive?" Natalia said. "You mean…"

She could not breathe.

All of the air had been sucked from her lungs, and she wondered if her soldier had felt the same way upon finding her body.

"Yes, Natalia, you are dead."

"But I can go back, right?"

The girl shifted. "Technically, no, but technically, yes. You see, I am not supposed to send people back to where they came from…but there was clearly a mistake made during the explosion, as you should have survived the blast."

"Can you send me back?"

The girl sighed, then tucked a strand of platinum hair behind her ear. Waving her hand, a control board appeared. She typed a few things, then looked up. "Are you sure?"

Natalia hesitated, but then chastised herself for waiting. "Of course."

"Hold on."

The girl pressed a button, and Natalia felt a sensation she could not describe, like being pushed and pulled all at the same time. Then stars clouded her vision, and as simply as it had started, it ended.

part three.

in which two are allowed a second chance at fate, and the story goes on.

Air filled her lungs as she gasped for breath. Although her throat burned and her chest hurt, nothing was sweeter than the oxygen that she inhaled so desperately.

His eyes shot open, looking down at the body in his arms. Tear stains marked his cheeks, a telltale sign of sorrow. "Natalia?"

Pain was a sense that became overwhelmingly clear. It racked her whole body, and she wondered if she could even talk without fumbling her words. She had a throbbing headache and every single muscle was sore.

Her dark eyes searched upwards, finding him. It wasn't hard. She knew her ankle was probably broken judging by the pain that shot through her foot, but she was okay so long as he was there. "Sebastian," she exhaled, her voice sounding hoarse. She cleared her throat, but that didn't help much.

"Natalia," he gasped. "You're alive…"

She tried to sit up, but she let out an involuntary groan when attempting to.

"Don't move," he said. "I think you broke something, I'm not sure what. We have to get you to a hospital…"

She nodded as best as she could. "I- ah- it was an explosion, right?"

His eyes met hers and he gave her a single nod in response.

dear new york.

"Did...did anyone die?"

He hesitated, and her heart dropped. But he shook his head, and relief flooded her. "No."

"Thank God."

She sat up again, despite the pain that screamed at her not to move.

"Don't-" he started, but seeing that she was already up he decided not to argue.

Natalia winced at the throbbing pain that shot down her spine. Although she doubted that any bones in her actual spine were broken, she suspected that she might've pulled a muscle (or several) and would have bruises everywhere.

She felt something sticky dripping down her left arm, and her eyes drifted to figure out the problem. A piece of metal was wedged in her arm. It wasn't a big piece, but there was no telling how far it was stuck, or if it went in crooked or bent.

"You need some help," Sebastian said, his voice serious. He stood up, and leaned down to help her stand. She cried out when she put pressure on her right ankle, so he shifted. "Don't walk on that leg," he said. He put his arm around her to support her, and he helped her get back to the transit vehicle they were using.

The pilot in the small helicopter nearly passed out at seeing the extent of Natalia's wounds, but Sebastian just told him to take the pair to the hospital.

As soon as they arrived, Sebastian got out of the copter and carried Natalia inside. The emergency room was full of people, mostly those waiting for loved ones to come out. Since her outward appearance was so ragged from the explosion, she was seen mere minutes after entering.

"What is her name?" a nurse asked Sebastian.

"Natalia Alice Abernathy," he said, his voice quiet and anxious. He had been asked to wait in the designated waiting room after refusing treatment for his minor scrapes and bruises.

Time seemed to drag by unbelievably slowly. He could not help but worry every second that passed.

"Mr. Gulinov?" a female voice in the hallway said. He looked up, alert.

"Yes?"

"Natalia is all fixed up. We would like to have her stay overnight in order to monitor her vitals to make sure she stays stable. If you would like to visit her, you may do so now."

He stood up. A glance at his watch told him he had been idly waiting for three and a half hours. He sighed. That couldn't be healthy, but he was glad no one had objected to him while he had been in that state.

"Natalia," he said, entering the room. "How are you?"

She looked up, her frizzy hair pulled back and dark eyes tired. "Better than before."

He sat down on the edge of her bed. "You...back in Maine, in the city, you actually died. I was there. I felt it. You had no heartbeat. How are you alive?"

He didn't mean for it to come out as blunt as it did, and he immediately regretted his choice of words. But she did not seemed fazed.

"I was given a choice."

"A...choice?"

The very idea confused him.

"Yes. Between life and death. A girl appeared; she said that I was not supposed to die and I could choose. The place was white, but there were shadows down one corridor."

"And you chose life over death? Pain over freedom? Heartbreak over happiness?"

dear new york.

She shook her head, a slight smile gracing her lips, her eyes bright. "You do not understand. I did not choose life."

He tilted his head to the side in confusion, and she did not drop her smile for a second.

"I chose you."

dear new york.

Letters, III. "To The Boy Who Works At The Lego Store".

I have a question.

I'll keep this brief, and know that you are not required to answer should you feel uncomfortable doing so. However, there are some things I need to say.

Why do you ignore me?

I don't mean when we see each other face to face, for you seem to go out of your way to speak to me if you meet me in public. Remember when we ran into each other at the thrift store a few weeks ago? I didn't even know you were there, but you called my name from across the room just to say hello. And, every time I come into your workplace, you maintain eye contact with me from over the counter until one of us is persuaded into saying something.

But when I text you, you never respond.

Perhaps I have the wrong phone number. You could have changed it - that happens all the time. But I know for a fact I have your correct social media because your girlfriend tags you in everything, and you like her posts.

Why do you ignore me?

I sound crazy.

I sound like some creep who stalks you all the time and demands answers, but it's just a soft question. No answer necessary, no stress, no requirements. Just a question, from someone sincerely confused and someone who wishes to be your friend.

Sincerely, Em.

dear new york.

Poetry, III. "2008".

congratulations, i've been officially lied to.

so this must be exactly how that feels.

congratulations, your deception is bulletproof.

i wonder if these wounds will ever heal.

> i can't believe you thought it'd end in a parade of pity tears.

> i can't believe you have the guts to turn this all on us.

>> and honestly, i thought you'd stay, but now i wish you'd go.

can we go back to a time when

> no one told any lies

>> and we were silently, blissfully ignorant?

can we go back to 2008?

> can we get past what it takes

>> to reconcile our lives, quietly, stubbornly innocent?

dear new york.

Contemplations, I.

The drive bores me.

    Every day, I follow the same route to school, to work, to church.

    Every day, I take University to 31, and exit Sylacauga.

    Every day, I follow Oxmoor Road from Homewood.

    Every day, I am tired.

    Is there some way to break this rote pattern of repetition? I am forever stuck in this cycle of commute that has been normalized. Why must I drive in these circles?

    As someone who prides herself in always testing the boundaries of the world, I am unsure how to venture past the drive.

    It is true there are many routes, but they all end up at the same location.

    Will I break the barriers by next September?

    We'll find out.

    I hope to high heavens I can move on, for if I am stuck in this circle for much longer, I may become eternally attached to it, and render myself lacking of independence.

dear new york.

Letters, IV. "Dear Future Lover".

Dear future lover,

    Where are you now?

    I know you're out there somewhere in the world.

    Are you with someone else now? Or are you like me, always wondering when and where your other half will appear?

    I have heard stories of the relationships people get into when they are too young. The truth is, I may be too young, or perhaps I am just too busy. With school, a part-time job, and an internship, my schedule is always full.

    I can make time, though.

    Where are you now?

    If you dare, show up in my life. Make yourself known, so I know what to look forward to. Even if you and I are not meant to be right now, I can't help but wonder who you may be. You are a mystery now, a stranger. Perhaps I don't even know you yet. Perhaps you will attend the same college I will, or maybe I have met you before.

    Where are you now?

    Only time will tell.

    Nothing that I can say or do will allow me to meet you sooner, for fate has its timing in some sort of special way. Between you and I, I think it's a little unfair for me to keep waiting, but wait I will. Are you near me now, or are you off in some other state or country?

dear new york.

  Wherever you may be, know that I am looking forward to meeting you more than I could ever express. There is something so exciting about the possibility of love, especially for one that has yet to feel anything beyond the sting of lost childhood crushes.

  Where are you now?

dear new york.

Short, III. "The Truth, Amongst Other Things".

"We used to be friends." I say, with resolve in my tone. Ben and I are standing in front of a fire pit, a box of matches in my hand and assorted items of Val's amongst the kindling.

Ben turns his head to look at me. "Used to?"

"Yeah. I always went to her family's house for Thanksgiving dinner, and it was one night in particular when it all fell apart."

"Hey, Ronnie! Come on in."

"Their family was always super nice to me, but this year, they seemed hostile."

I took a seat at the table, and everyone watched me with a side eye. It was as if I had done something terribly wrong - only I didn't know what it was.

"Later that evening, Val pulled me aside and let me know that she told her parents I was the one who gave her a pack of cigarettes two weeks prior."

"Was it you?" Ben asks, curious.

"God, no. I'm not like that." I pause. "Why, do you think I am?"

Ben looks as if he wants to say something, but he keeps his mouth shut.

Probably for the best.

"Veronica, we need to talk to you." It was Val's parents, after dinner ended. I was helping clear the table as always. There, in front of everyone, her father sternly talked to me. "We can't believe you gave Val cigarettes. That was immature, irresponsible, and illegal. She's a good kid, and we thought you were too. If you keep influencing her like this, we can't let you be friends with her anymore."

Her mother chimed in. "We can't let her spend time with you when you're bound to end up in jail. Encouraging our daughter to break the law? I just can't believe you'd do something like this."

dear new york.

I couldn't let myself be pushed around like this. "Mr. and Mrs. Johnson, your daughter is my best friend. I never have and never will give her cigarettes... in fact, I don't smoke them myself and I never have. Your daughter lied to you. I don't know why."

Her parents looked mortified. The whole room went silent. When someone finally spoke, it was her mother, in a quiet voice with a dangerous edge. "How dare you."

Val was standing in the archway separating the kitchen from the dining room. Her father turned to her.

"Valerie. Did she or did she not give you the cigarettes?"

"I can't believe she had the audacity to turn her mistakes on me."

"She did," Val says. No hesitation. No regret.

Her parents turned to face me, and with a solemn glare, her father said, "Get out."

I turned and left, overwhelmed with emotion. I called my dad to pick me up from their driveway. He arrived, and I wouldn't say a word on the way back.

"Wow," Ben says, in a little shock.

"Yeah," I say. I shake my head. "Don't mess with her. She'll stab you in the back and apologize while you bleed out."

I strike the match and throw it into the pit.

dear new york.

A Brief Intermission To Discuss Politics.

(Never Fear, This Letter Is Unbiased.)

I am seventeen. I cannot vote. But, chances are, you can.

Dear America, please vote. There are people in charge that should not be because of the lack of voters in past elections. If everyone between the ages of eighteen and twenty-five registered, they would hold the popular vote in the polls.

Voting is often taken for granted in this country. We are one of the select few nations in the world that allow people of all colors, religions, and genders to vote. Of course, there are some changes that could be made to better the system, but we often don't realize what we have sitting in front of us. In 2016, many people didn't vote because of work obligations or because they believed their vote would be futile in the long run. The truth is that your vote is your voice.

The deadlines are always approaching. Go online, check the registration deadline for your state, and get to the polls. Research the candidates. Take voting day as seriously as you possibly can - it is the day that you weigh in on the future of our country. Have you ever found yourself sitting at home watching the news and wondering why so many terrible things are happening? Vote in someone that has the ability and the motivation to change something for the better! Have you ever passed election signs in your neighborhood, but discovered you didn't know any of the names? Educate yourself! There are so many sites and informative articles that give you the basics of each candidate, including their believes, their history with politics, and their party. Remember, though - you don't have to vote for someone because they are a part of the party you most identify with the beliefs of! Vote for who you want in office.

No pressure.

dear new york.

No stress.

No worries.

Your vote is yours, completely confidential. Your preferences are never shared unless you discuss that with your friends or family, and even then, it's your choice to share that information. No one is judging you for who you mark on the ballot.

Get out there, America.

Please.

Vote.

The future of the nation depends on it.

dear new york.

Poetry, IV. "Seismic".

> *I once wrote a short story with this plot.*
>
> *I adapted the story into a poem, and this is the final edit.*

It's hard to keep up with the noises in your head.
> It's a long and winding road to walk the path that you have lead.
>> I wish I could say that I'll miss you, but I won't,
> your rainbows of color fading into crimson red.

It's hard to give it up when you wanted more.
> How many other lies have you told before?
>> I wish I could say that I miss you, but I don't.

You left me all alone, and I survived a war.
>> You say it's my fault we're through,
>>> as if anything you've said has been true,
>>>> and if these fault lines could crack the waves would be seismic.

> Go run from me, far away,
> it's not my fault, and I'll be okay.
> Go run from all the bad decisions you made,
>> if anyone could truly love you, I'd believe they're insane.

dear new york.

Poetry, V. "Static".

the noise is too loud for my head
    and i've kept my glass in my hand
        though i've wanted to smash it on several separate occasions.
my mother goes on and on about how to love people,
    but she doesn't realize her words are
        rote,
            repetitive,
                reiterated.
i am a girl made of steel and of words and of fire
    yet i am a glass pane meant to shatter against the rough terrain.
        has everything i have ever known been a lie?
            or is this reality the one i have been searching for?
        his voice is deep like a bass note.
i've always liked the radio
    but it is as if i am between stations,
        some tuning that has not yet been occupied by music.
            i have been music before,
        and i will be music again,
    yet i fail to see the silver lining
through the static.

dear new york.

Poetry, VI. "Definition".

You are not defined by your failure.

You are not defined by the mistakes

    you've made,

    are making,

    and will make.

You are not defined by

    your sadness

    or your anger

    or your rage.

You are not limited to the highest point you've ever reached.

You are not head back by the heaviness that weighs the world down.

        You are free.

dear new york.

Poetry, VII.

tomorrow will be better.

    i know it's cold right now and it seems that nothing can change the weather.

tomorrow will be better.

        no matter what storms lie ahead,

            i promise you it's all in your head.

dear new york.

Contemplations, II. "Thoughts & Prayers".

Little girl, only seventeen,

    wants her face in a magazine.

Her father says it's just a dream

        and she'll wake up in the morning.

            Oh, America, what have we done?

            That morning was the last time she saw the sun.

Little boy, fourteen years of age,

    wants to fly a ship to space.

His mother says he's got to get good grades,

        and he thinks the chance to see the stars is worth the wait.

            Oh, America, what have we done?

            Children should never stare down the barrel of a gun.

            Are we through with these games we play?

            Someone do something besides think and pray.

            He's never going to fly that ship to space.

dear new york.

Poetry, VIII. "Prologue".

    I CAN SEE IT NOW:

JANUARY 2012, A COOL BREEZE, BEFORE THE WORLD ENDED IN DECEMBER.

THAT WAS FAR TOO LONG AGO

    I'M STUDYING THE ARTS OVERSEAS

        AND 2012'S THE YEAR NO ONE REMEMBERS.

    REMEMBER WHEN THE TABLES TURNED

AND WE TRIED TO SIT DOWN ANYWAY AND HAVE DINNER?

WE WERE A NAIVE PEOPLE

    WE WERE INSANE

        AND HERE WE ARE, OPENING THE FISSURE.

    REMEMBER IN 2012

WHEN THE WORLD WAS NICE, WHEN WE HAD OUR HEADS ON STRAIGHT?

WHEN WE SAID A PRAYER

    AND NOW

        WE STAND IN THE RUBBLE?

    REMEMBER IN 2012

WHEN OUR BIGGEST FEARS WEREN'T OF MONSTERS OR OF WAVES?

REMEMBER WHEN WE DIDN'T PUT

    CHILDREN IN GRAVES?

        AND NOW

            WE STAND IN THE RUBBLE.

dear new york.

Poetry IX. "Sunday Evening".

It smells like rain outside.

    The lights in my room have a purple glow.

        The sounds of the television plays in the living room.

            My sister is resting after sports practice.

                The puppy is taking a nap - sometimes I wish I was the puppy.

            Will it rain when I go to the movies tonight?

        Will I see my coworkers while I am out?

    Will I meet anyone worthwhile?

        It is a Sunday evening.

            November is warm, as usual.

                The southern winters never fail to disappoint,

            leaves still on the trees from months ago.

    It is as if autumn never began.

        I work the early shift tomorrow.

            Sunday evenings don't last forever,

        but I wish they would.

dear new york.

Contemplations, III. "Fog".

The fog rolls over the hills at six-thirty in the morning.

    I am on my way to work when I see the waves approaching, cold and dreary. They excite me, though.

    Sunny days and warm weather aren't my type. I belong in a city with fog and with wind and with rain.

    It is storming now, the evening hours upon me. It is dark outside. Night has fallen.

    Mid-mornings and brunches aren't my type. I belong in a world with late night phone calls and with stargazing and with long talks when the lights are off.

    When the fog rolls over the hills at six-thirty tomorrow,

                            I will drive on.

dear new york.

Short, IV. "Frame".

His boots were falling apart, but that was how he liked them. He thought it gave him an edgy look, some sort of indie expectation that he was allowing himself to try and live up to. He would always take pictures in those boots, camera focused on the trees in the distance, the depth of the greenery captivating. No one ever took photos of him, though. The photographer was never showed in the moments he froze in a frame.

I noticed him, when no one else did. His dark hair fell to to his shoulders because he refused to cut it. He wore dark clothing, but his personality was neon if someone was willing to take the chance to get to know him.

"Blair," he said successfully getting my attention. The moment I turned to look at him, he snapped a photo of me, causing me to roll my eyes. He'd done that more than one time.

The thing was, we were both lost.

Not in a physical way, but in a metaphorical way. You know, the way they talk about in television shows, to sound fancy or theoretical. But this was a real sense of feeling out-of-place, and we shared the experience. We skipped school days just because it was nice outside and the sunflowers beckoned us to their paradise. We searched for the little things, things that didn't belong, things that we could relate to. The irrelevancy of a speed limit sign. The indecency of a car parked improperly.

He always said he wanted to make a difference. Do something with his life. I don't think he knew what he was asking for: something impossible. It was like trying to capture a photo of the stars on a cell phone camera. It was like trying to reach your destination on time in rush hour traffic. It was like holding back the rain.

dear new york.

Sebastian was the rain.

He knew he was a force of nature, he could feel it in his bones. He was on fire, and no one understood that except for him. He could burn his way through the northern forests and not even flinch. He was a tidal wave, sweeping over the coastal cities.

But he was drowning in himself. He didn't have anywhere to go, no escape from the waters except when he was out taking pictures. He was a storm, and he was destroying himself in the process. He needed help, even if he didn't want to admit it.

I remember the first time we went out to the fields of yellow and green. He hardly spoke, and on the way back, he was in the passenger seat of my car, going through the photos he'd taken. He had an eye for beauty, but he failed to see himself as a subject of mystery and intrigue. Sometimes I wish I would've been a better friend before he started flirting with death, not after. The things he would do in order to get a good photo far surpassed his conscience. He snuck into restricted areas, and made close calls with law enforcement on multiple occasions. That wasn't all, though…because he had nothing to lose, he would dare to lean over the edges of cliffs, or stand next to a fast-moving body of water. There was no regard for safety. And he was so lost, he couldn't even see through the blur of right and wrong.

So when Sebastian Montague left town and never came back, I wasn't surprised in the least. I wished he had written a note or called me at least once, just to explain, but he was never one to pick up the phone. I asked the few friends he had, but they were more of acquaintances, and never knew who Sebastian really was.

All that remains of him in my life is the photo I have of him, behind a frame. I hope that's not all that's left of him, just a memory, but I don't have a way of knowing otherwise. So

dear new york.

in the frame he shall stay, until the photo fades or the glass breaks or he comes back, whichever comes first.

dear new york.

Short, V. "North Carolina".

She lives in North Carolina.

    The girl I like, that is.

    She's funny, and she's adorable. She has little antics that make me smile, and there's patterns in the way she texts. I can almost imagine her speaking the words that she sends me.

    In a perfect world, we would be together.

    At least, I like to think that.

    In reality, she probably wouldn't think of me. In a perfect world, she would be with someone who would treat her right, and that may not be me. In a perfect world, I would get accepted to the college of my dreams, and she might not attend near there.

    She writes music.

    So do I.

    Perhaps sometime our songs will collide into the same story, and people will wonder if we ever met.

    I make up these stories in my head, daydreams about different versions of myself that I wish I was. There is something about falling in love that makes one ache for the unknown and for the distant, the things we know we can never have. We are all searching for one thing but yet not every can receive it because of the way the world works.

    Why does the earth turn like this?

    Hues of red and blue paint my dreams as I sleep, colors that I know well. We have been taught that the world is black and white but with her, I have the gift of color. People will try to

dear new york.

tell me that love isn't real but it is and this is proof - that one being, absorbed in oneself, may perceive the world differently because of someone else.

    She is my world.

    If only I was within reach.

    She is too far away.

    Alas, we are separated, and we have yet to be reunited. Have the barriers that we put up become too much to tear down? We are strangers in passing universes, extending our hands to one another in hopes they meet. We are only as close as we allow ourselves to become.

    Years of heartache have taught us to pull away.

    Does she think of me?

    I doubt she ever writes things like these down, taking notes in black ink. I doubt she enjoys my company as much as I enjoy hers, and I doubt she has that same dopamine rush when she gets a text of mine.

    Yet here I sit, 12:19 a.m., wondering if this girl could ever love me back. I wrote a love letter in July to a beauty I met in New York and she never responded. I tossed my feelings out in the crowded city air, but they were returned to me. Mine to keep. Tucked in my pocket, longing to be let out, but never allowed to. Why must I hide what I have?

    Time will be kind to her, for she is full of grace and beauty and carries herself with some sort of dignity that I have only seen in few people before. She never falters. She sticks to what she believes, even when times get rough, even when it feels like life is telling her that she is not good enough. If only she understood that I will always be there to support her.

    No matter what, allies.

    Frankly, the distance may be what we need.

dear new york.

After all, we are strangers.

These are thoughts.

North Carolina is exactly 585 miles away.

She lives on in the future, and I write midnight letters in the present.

The world spins on, and the clock keeps ticking. I put down my pen, for it is too late to retire these feelings but also too late to continue a reiteration of a longing letter that is mediocre at best.

                                                                                        dear new york.

Poetry, X. "Stop".

      oh, dear, what have i done?

          there is something

              about your smile

                  that makes my heart

                                            stop.

i have been overwhelmed

      by all of you

          and I find myself

              utterly in love.

                                        why

                                  are you

                      all i have ever wanted?

        please set me free

dear new york.

Contemplations, IV. "Limitless".

I limit myself because I believe I am not enough.

    Do you find yourself doing the same?

    Constantly trying to impress people who do not matter and do not truly care about you?

    I find myself locking away that room in my mind with the truth inside. I do not know as much about me as I should and I have no one to blame for my lack of self-trust other than myself.

    It feels like my life is a different remix of every sob story ever. Family trouble. Sibling rivalries. Parents arguing in the living room. I'm seventeen and I want to scream in an open field, ruin my voice just to express how I feel with no one but the wildflowers to hear me. I'm tired of complaining to my friends. I'm tired of ranting in pathetic letters or subtweeting on social media.

    Let me be who I am.

    Promise me that no matter what happens, I am allowed to be who I have locked away. Promise me that I can be free for once, I can speak for once, I can dream for once. My thoughts have ascended to the heavens before and I only wish for them to rise once more. May I have permission to explore my own mind? To give myself labels where I see fit or to leave them off if I so desire? I am not some girl who will bow to the will of a man, nor am I so uptight that I will not resolve situations with others.

    The day I lose my confidence in my voice is the day I truly lose sight of who I am.

    I know who I am.

    The problem is, I don't know if I'm ready to show you.

dear new york.

    You will find me and tell me why I am wrong, and you will try to fix my mistakes. You will point out the flaws in my system and hand me parts that may not work with my machine to try to solve what you think is an issue. Perhaps it is not an issue. Perhaps it is a part of my identity. I am allowed to give myself an identity based on who I am. I know who I am.

    There is something in this world that has made me afraid before. Few people know my secrets. Few people can be trusted not to share them with the world when I don't want to explain to everyone I know why I am the way that I am.

    All you need to know is that I am me.

    All I have ever been is me.

    And whether or not that fits your mold is none of your concern.

    I limit myself because I believe I am not enough. When the time comes, when I make peace with myself, and when I finally stop feeling sorry for myself, I will be limitless.

    Only then will you find it completely and utterly impossible to drag me down.

dear new york.

A Thought, I.

why did you block me?

what did i ever do to you?

dear new york.

Short, VI. "Pretty Boys, Pretty Girls".

There are so many pretty boys.

Elise sat at the coffee shop with a paper cup in her right hand and her phone in her left. Casually texting, she noticed him from across the room.

He was perfect.

He was talking with one of his friends, and they laughed in a good-natured way. His eyes caught hers from a distance, and she averted hers quickly. She had never been one to maintain eye contact.

His shoulder brushed hers on the way out the door, and she watched him leave. If she was confident enough, perhaps she would talk to him. Perhaps she would find love like all of her friends had. They were always talking about their great adventures with their lovers, like how they snuck out in the evenings or how they wrote songs about one another.

This perfect boy was just another beautiful stranger in a coffee shop.

Disappointed in her lack of confidence, Elise drowned her temporary sorrows in espresso.

It looked like fall outside. It was November, veering on the edge of winter, but the trees were still changing colors, some still standing green as the solitary reminders of the summer that once had been.

When she left the coffee shop that day, her sadness over the loss of the beautiful stranger had been subdued, reduced to simple thoughts in the back of her mind. She would think about him, but she would forget what he looked like, and even if his face appeared in her dreams, she would have no remembrance of who he really was, only who her mind made him out to be. She had no true attachment to him, for she did not know him.

There are so many things that teenagers should not do.

Peter knew of these things, because he did them.

Every Friday, he would leave school early with his friends and smoke cigarettes in the parking lot behind the football field. The sad thing about it was that he had no conscience. None of it bothered him.

His best friend, Evan, would always talk about the girls he slept with. He bragged about it as a young boy would brag about winning a sports trophy. Peter would laugh and ask him about it, just to egg him on. There was no remorse.

Whenever his parents went to church on Sundays, Peter would stay back to "do homework". By homework, he meant that he would go over to Evan's to smoke and discuss girls. They would listen to classic rock and pretend like they were a part of bands like The Romantics.

One Sunday afternoon, Peter was bored, so he dragged Evan to a coffee shop. The pair stole Evan's father's keys and drove the new Cadillac to the quaint place. It was down the street, and it had just opened up. As they walked up, they pointed out flaws in the architecture and mocked the modern rustic style that it had.

As the pair stood in line, they whispered crude remarks about a woman standing in front of them. Upon ordering, Peter put on sugar-coated manners while Evan messed with the barista on purpose. After they got their drinks, Peter noticed a pretty girl looking at him from across the small coffee shop.

She was perfect.

She was by herself, and she appeared to be checking text messages or something of the sort. She had a cup of coffee in her hand, just like him. Evan made a quiet joke about the condition of the coffee shop floors, and the pair laughed.

Peter made eye contact with the girl.

She looked away. He knew how girls responded to his good looks, so he used it to his advantage, making a remark at Evan.

On the way out, he brushed her shoulder on purpose. He knew without having to look back that she watched him leave. Evan started the engine to the borrowed Cadillac and pulled out of the parking spot, heading back to the neighborhood they lived in.

Peter was not the perfect boy Elise thought he was.

dear new york.

A Thought, II. "Tribute To A Meme".

WHAT IS

FATE IN *BEOWULF*,

YOU MAY ASK?

dear new york.

Letters, V. "To An Icon".

To an icon:

    I hope you're doing well in heaven.

    How is it up there? Is it as bright and as extravagant as you would have liked?

    You were a legend, and you knew it. People told you, and you walked out the lifestyle you wanted to. No one told you what to do. I admire that.

    There is nothing that I can write that other people haven't already said about you. Despite your bad days, you carried the weight of a generation with you. So many people grew up listening to the music you wrote, my parents included. When I was a kid, I used to hear your songs on the radio. Obviously, you weren't the only one to be credited for the music, but you were the most outstandingly brave.

    You helped me to understand who I am.

    You were so extra that it makes me so much more confident - if you could do it, I can too. Thank you for being who you were.

    Thank you for being yourself.

    Sincerely,

        just a girl.

dear new york.

Letters, VI. "Caitlin".

You are the perfect friend.

    My heart jumps when I get a text from you, because you are so important to my life.

    In November 2016, I was just a weary sophomore with a foot injury. Hobbling around an Atlanta hotel on crutches, I met you. Ever since that day, you have been the one person from our friend group that stayed in touch with me. You are also the one person that I have been able to see again since our separation. Nothing has been as fun as going to Chinatown to get dumpling and rolled ice cream with you.

    Your home city impresses me. Sometimes I can't believe that you live there - for me to live there would be a dream, and you live it. I can only hope I can move there and meet you again for coffee on weekends. I'll help you write college essays, and you can help me become fully acquainted with New York.

    Your sister is so talented. I can't wait to watch her on Broadway in ten years. Whatever path life takes her on, I hope she knows that she is so loved and worthy.

    You matter so much to me. Even if you ever feel like no one else cares, I care. No matter how angry or sad or disappointed I may see, you will always matter to me. You are the one person in my life for the past two years that I have been able to constantly count on. Whether we are crying over the same movies from thousands of miles apart or texting about Roger Taylor, you are so much fun to talk to. I love your humor, and I love your personality.

    Never let anyone tell you that you are not important, because you are. Never let anyone treat you as less than the queen that you are. Beyond your beauty and your stellar personality, you are a positive influence and you have the power to change the world. I will be your right hand man in all of your endeavors, should you need one. If you ever need anyone to talk to, just call me.

No matter where I am, and no matter where you are, you will be my priority.

Here's to more years of friendship and happiness and personal discovery. May we both find our loves, wherever they may be. May we both carry on as we have thus far. And, beyond that, may we both be who we want to be.

I miss you, and I love you.

dear new york.

Poetry, XI. "Tea".

the stage is set: you and i,

        one of us is telling a lie.

we are warriors, both of us,

        but only one can survive.

the stage is set: you and me,

        don't pretend to be my friend.

we are done, this is it,

        meet me at the end.

                          who will break the other first?

                        out of cruel things, who said the worst?

                          who will break the other first?

               in this vast world of accusations, who said the worst?

    it's just dramatics

        it's just rage

           it's just gossip

                it's just hate

                    it's only words

                        it's only small talk

                            and here's the tea.

dear new york.

Letters, VII. "To A Legend".

To a legend:

    I am sorry you have gone.

    November 12, 2018.

    You passed in a hospital in Los Angeles. My condolences to your family, by the way - they will miss you far more than I ever could.

    For years, you introduced us to our favorite heroes. You are an iconic symbol in film and in comics, and I will always remember you. My siblings and I used to hunt for your cameo in films, and would laugh at your appearances. You always lightened the mood.

    The world was blessed to have you.

    I hope you are finally reunited with your wife after a long year of being apart. You were both ninety-five at your passing, but despite that age, you are immortal.

    Thank you for all you have done.

dear new york.

Poetry, XII. "In".

i was lost and you were found,
      neon nights set ablaze.
lovers buried in the ground, swallowed by the graveyard haze.
the war's over, but you're still mad,
      because we went our separate ways.
but you're still my olympiad, forever lost in a mental maze.

            \

      our love is always in,
there is no going out.
      but i don't mind a bit when we're laying on your couch.
      our love is always in,
no need for you to pout
you know you'll always win, don't ever have a doubt about it,

                          darling,

                                we're in.

dear new york.

Letters, VIII. "Ariel".

Dear best friend,

    you are the Joey to my Chandler.

    (Granted, we both know that I'm more of a Monica, but all truths aside, you complete me.)

    I first saw you at a little school on the Upper West Side, cramped into those horrendous closets they called dorm rooms. I first met you on 61st Street, where we took lessons in acting. I first began to know you in the studio space we adopted as a cafeteria for those two weeks and on the bus where we sang Disney show theme songs at the top of our lungs.

    Congratulations on getting into college, by the way - you know I am so proud of you. I may have only been living the same life as you for two weeks, but I am eternally grateful for everything you taught me.

    Loyalty.

    Peace.

    Confidence.

    You are all of those things and more.

    Meet me in Alabama? You and I, one more adventure?

dear new york.

Contemplations, V. "That Could Have Been Me".

That could have been me.

I almost went to that mall the night of the shooting. Sometimes I get in arguments with ignorant people. Sometimes I go too far; that could have been me.

What if I stood up for myself?

What if that person got angry?

What if they had a weapon? That's legal.

What if they decided that their honor was worth more than my life?

We live in America, ladies and gentlemen, and this is our reality.

In school, we notice the kids that don't fit in much because we have to be aware of our surroundings.

When we hear of another school shooting, we think, that could have been me.

No political views. No opinions. Just the truth.

We have allowed this disgusting act of murder to become the norm. There have been 320 shootings this year. It's November 25th.

Rise up, youth. No one else will.

dear new york.

Poetry, XIII. "Hymn To The 42".

    second guessing myself's become a habit

        comes naturally when she's around

    mad that i can't do anything about it

        dig a hole, bury myself in the ground

                you don't really know me at all.

dear new york.

Poetry, XIV. "Vulcan".

The Roman god of the forges illuminates the sky of my hometown,

    piercing through the veil of fog,

        casting shadows from the light he produces.

The torch in his hand is ever-glowing,

    always aflame.

        He watches the magic city below.

            The man appeared long ago, and has only once left our hilltop.

Like an old friend, he stands above us

    next to the radio towers which are young compared to him.

        The timeless man of the fires and the forgery

            guards the city of unpredictable weather,

                unpredictable people,

                    and unpredictable years.

    Despite the frail promises, Vulcan remains.

dear new york.

Letters, IX. "To My Friends".

To my friends from July:

    You mean so much to me.

    Though I haven't the time nor the energy to write an individual letter to all of you, I will do my best to give you each a paragraph or a moment. Remember, you are so much more than just a few sentences - I could never write a novel with all of the things I love about each of you.

    In no particular order, we begin.

    To London. You are a talented individual that absolutely blew my mind upon our first meeting. No one would imagine that so much raw talent and acting power would fit inside someone so small, but you are the impossible. You continue to impress me every day.

    To Jess. You have matured since I began to know you, and that's incredible, because it hasn't been long. Not only have you matured mentally, but you have matured as an actress, and I cannot wait to see where your new knowledge takes you. You can always call me.

    To Lisa. Do I need to write to you? You know how much I appreciate you. And, if you don't, here we go: you are kind, funny, generous, and one of my best friends. You can talk to me whenever, because you are so special to me.

    To Bren. You were my stage brother, and that's the closest we've gotten - but I'd say family's pretty close. Carry on in life, and be the person I know you are destined to become.

    To Mac. You're my best friend (and apparently I'm your second best friend). Self-explanatory. I still have your plastic spoon.

    To Ariel. Honey, you got a letter. I was inspired. Go back a few pages.

dear new york.

To Lori. You are a future Marvel star, and I'll cast you when I write a film for them. You are so talented, and a fashion icon. We need to meet up for lunch sometime. Meet halfway? Tennessee isn't that bad, right?

To Claire. In my eyes, you were one of the best actors at AMDA this summer. You absolutely killed your role, and you have the amazing ability to easily shift from character to character. You're going far, Georgia.

To Wisocky. When I first saw you in the room we adopted as our lunchroom, I wondered if I would be your friend. Most acting classes end up dividing into little cliques, but I was thrilled when our group became a close-knit family. You are incredibly talented. Send me tickets to your shows and premieres, or you're fired.

To Vincenzo. Your scene with Wisocky made me laugh so hard, time and time again. You are a wonderful actor and a delight to work with (even if we never had a scene together). I know I'll remember you.

To Mia B. Oh my goodness, I love you. You're so sweet, and your humor is just my type. You never fail to make me smile. When you get bored with Singapore, please fly to me. I need a coffee break with you to catch up.

To Mia P. You are an actress I'll definitely be keeping up with, because I know you're going far. Nothing can change my mind about that. Wherever you choose to go to college, they'll be incredibly lucky to have you!

To Brian. I can't pick favorite stage brothers, but you're up there. Juilliard would be missing out if they didn't accept you… but if they don't, I know you'll go somewhere that will make you into the best actor you can be.

dear new york.

To Jason. Despite our tiny disagreement, you're a cool guy. You educated me on New York City street sizes and names, and for that I am eternally grateful.

To Ashleigh. I'm sorry we made fun of you for not taking the subway after that one time you got lost. All in all, I think you're incredibly brave to ever travel the city by yourself, and you're an amazing actor (and it's even more amazing that you haven't acted before!). Call me up anytime!

To Liz. I love that you love Disney so much. You're full of joy, and that makes you fun to be around. You're always positive, and I adore that about you. You're a great scene partner, and you're easy to work with!

To Sophie. Never give up! I admire your persistence and your willingness to try new things. The first day we met, I got the impression that you would work hard at things, and you did. You did amazing in your performance, and you're going to do amazing in life!

To Charlie. I love your name and everything it stands for. I'm sorry I called you Kayla once, I still think about that. Your ability to feel emotions as a character impresses me so much - you have so much potential. I cannot wait to brag about the fact that I went to summer camp with you when you become rich and famous.

To the entire AMDA Acting group in session two - you mean so much to me, beyond what words can express. I know there are many reiterations in this letter, and I know there are too many mentions of "so" and "talented", but it's true. A reunion is very necessary.

dear new york.

Closure.

To everyone who read this book,

    thank you for allowing me to express my thoughts.

        I am just a teen girl in a big world, trying to find out who I am.

           I sit in a Starbucks closing this.

              With another sip of my mocha,

                  DEAR NEW YORK comes to an

                                END.

dear new york.

www.ingramcontent.com/pod-product-compliance
Lightning Source LLC
Chambersburg PA
CBHW030459220526
45464CB00006B/2585